Over, Under, Through

Jasmine Williams

BookLeaf Publishing

Over, Under, Through © 2023 Jasmine Williams

All rights reserved.

No part of this publication may be reproduced, stored in a retrieval system, or transmitted, in any form or by any means, electronic, mechanical, photocopying, recording, or otherwise, without the prior written permission of the presenters.

Jasmine Williams asserts the moral right to be identified as the author of this work.

Presentation by *BookLeaf Publishing*

Web: www.bookleafpub.com

E-mail: info@bookleafpub.com

ISBN: 9789357696197

First edition 2023

DEDICATION

To anyone out there who feels alone or undeserving:

You are incredible just the way you are. Never lose your light. Find something to make it burn brighter.

ACKNOWLEDGEMENT

There are so many people who deserve acknowledgment (good and bad) in my life, it's hard to even begin.

First, I want to thank my best friend for never leaving my side. You are the greatest and most inspiring friend a person could ask for. Thank you for being my poem reader, twin daydreamer, and life completer.

To my amazing mom: Thank you for giving me life and continuing to give me happiness every single day. You are my critical editor, constant motivator, and loving caretaker. I don't know what I'd do without you.

Special thanks to Big'm Chief for being the best book supporter of all time. You are the greatest. <3

To my whole family: I could never ask for a better one. You guys are my home, no matter where you are.

To fellow authors: There are so many writers out there who continue to inspire me every single day.

Reading your work continues to help me grow into myself. Thank you for all that you do.

To the people who've hurt me: Know that all that you have said and done has not left me broken. I'm still standing here today, chasing after my dreams. You have made me stronger and able to realize what I deserve in this world.

Finally, I want to thank the people at BookLeaf Publishing for giving me such an incredible opportunity to become a published author. None of this would have been possible without you.

PREFACE

Writing this book has truly allowed me to work through my struggles and dissect my thoughts. I have been in love with poetry since a very young age, starting with the timeless Emily Dickinson. Being able to further develop my love for writing while discovering parts of myself has been such an incredible journey that I can't wait to share.

Enough

No one ever says thank you
No one ever says good job
It's always "Put more effort in"
You're really looking like a slob
There're bags under your eyes
And you're in another mood
You're losing too much weight
Yet you're "always eating food"

Why are you always tired
And laying in your bed
Maybe it's the constant thoughts
Racing through my head
I want to be good enough
For each new expectation
Constantly searching for
Some kind of validation

I've lost my motivation
For things I loved before
I'm not that "little girl"
You knew so well before
I just wish that you could see
All the good that I have done
And I hope that one day soon
I'll finally be enough

No One Should

No one should be ashamed of who they are
Hiding out in alleyways or specialized bars
No one should be afraid of being seen
Called awful names like 'abomination" or "unclean"

No one should be scared to lose their home
Their family, their friends; all they've ever known
No one should feel bad for loving who they love
Yet each day, another person does

Slowly it's improving throughout our land
From the inhuman ways of uncivil hands
But still many suffer in "the land of the free"
And each day I wonder, "Why can't I just be me?"

Love is Like the Ocean

Love is like the ocean

There are still times when everything feels safe
And times when it is rough, like the waves of a roaring tsunami
It can knock you under or lift you up
You can float peacefully or be dragged along, sometimes without even knowing
It represents both unity and destruction, hope and fear

Love is like the ocean, and I feel like I'm drowning

An Eraser

I wish I was an eraser
Darkened with age
Dismantling my memories
Like words on a page
Not the good ones
Only the bad
So that maybe this way
I won't be quite as sad

I wish I was an eraser
Blurring the lines
Between good and bad
Between space and time
Creating a blank slate
To develop anew
Growing into myself
And not someone for you

I don't wish to be an eraser
Flaking off in shards

Breaking myself down
Into tiny little parts
Brushing away the pieces
And trampling them underfoot
Leaving nothing left
But dust and rubber soot

I don't wish to be an eraser
Slowly fading away
Because I know that soon
It will all be okay
I've learned to love myself
The way you never could
And now I don't pick out my flaws
But focus on the good

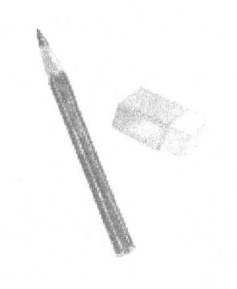

Air

I wish I was to someone else
What air is to my lungs
My absence leaves them breathless
But my presence fills them up
I'd surround them like a blanket
And be there all the time
Each night they'd say that I am theirs
The way that they are mine

I'm the air within their sails
That keeps their heart afloat
I'm the wind within a hurricane
That drowns them like a boat
I'm suffocating yet
They can't help but want for more
They're the boat lost out at sea
And I'm the safety of the shore

All the Things

I used to wish I was all the things
I know I'll never be
Happy, funny, pretty, smart
Not just somewhere in between
I'm done with being average
I know that name no more
Now I'm called extraordinary
And shall no longer be ignored

Some call me by nicknames
Like weird or odd or strange
All to hide the simple fact
That they're the ones deranged
I'm the one who broke their molds
And made one of my own
For extraordinary knows no bounds
And cannot be overthrown

Summer Leaf

I wish I was a Summer leaf
Blowing in the wind
Not caring where I'm going
Or caring where I end
Flying high without a care
Lost all on my own
Waiting till the day until
I find my way back home

I wish I was a Summer leaf
Floating in the breeze
Escaping from my troubles
With every bit of ease
Listening to the sounds of life
Swirling all around
Watching people from the air
But discarded on the ground

I don't wish to be a Summer leaf
Changing with Autumn's arrival

People sparring just a glance
Though my beauty is unrivaled
My touch the last glimpse
Of warmth within the air
One last effort to stop
The cold which we'll soon bear

I don't wish to be a Summer leaf
Dead when Winter comes
Wilted upon the frozen earth
And left completely numb
Wanting for those warmer days
Drifting beneath the sun
Longing to be loved again
Those Summer days redone

Fever Dream

Your fingers leave trails of fire
All along my skin
My whole body fills with burning desire
Imagining where you could have been
These feelings consume my thoughts
From day's beginning to day's end
So why is it so f****** hard
For me to simply let you in

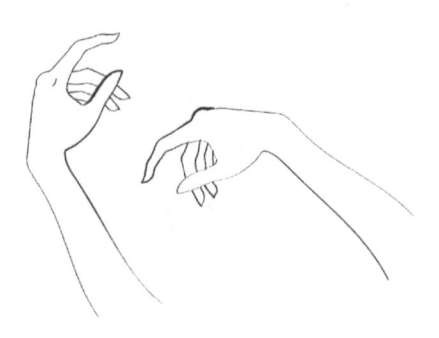

Phoenix

Life has left me
I'm here all alone
Soulless and empty
Heart hardened to stone

With skin turned to ashes
And mind black and bruised
This body was built
To be broken and used

My fire has burned up
Its heat is no more
Every piece of myself
Has been shattered and torn

Isn't this what you wanted
What you begged me to do

With such violent words
And your cruel point of view

Weren't you expecting
For me to grow once again
Even more vibrant
Than I was to begin

From those burnt ashes
That you trampled and crushed
My new spirit has risen
Completely untouched

My eyes can now shine
And my voice can now sing
Life has not left me
It has given me wings

Ghost

You act like this is normal
As if nothing's going on
How are you so sure
That you're never in the wrong

You're constantly degrading
My words and how I feel
With every day that passes
You act like I'm not real

Can't you see me standing here?
I'm right in front of you
Can't you feel my chilling pain
When I walk into a room

I'm shouting through the halls
And slamming all the doors
But no matter what I do
It is continually ignored

I'm just a ghost to you
Dead but still around
Tethered to your soul
Wishing to be unbound

Calling out to you
From the other side
If you can't communicate
Then please just say goodbye

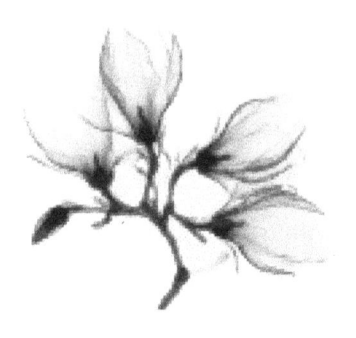

Little Bird

Peace be with you
The little bird said
Just seconds before
Its wings turned red

Why do we shoot
Without thinking first
Why can't we wait
To display our outbursts

The world would be better
If less blood was shed
That's what the little bird
Would have said

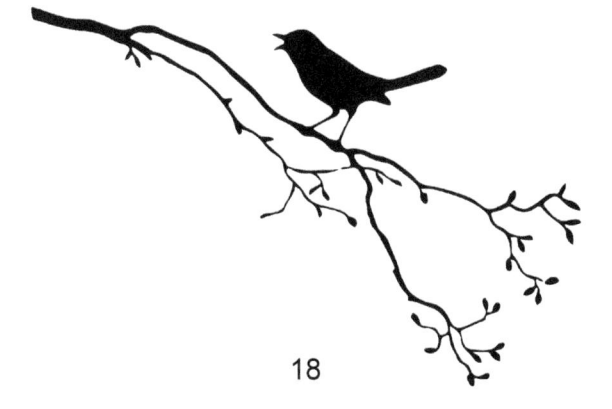

Crazy People

People say I'm crazy
Loving someone like you
Looking up in admiration
At all the stupid things you do

People say I'm crazy
For continuing to stay
Taking in your harsh words
While thinking it'll be okay

People say I'm crazy
Putting my heart on the frontline
Having no self-preservation
Letting you destroy my mind

People say I'm crazy
And I think they might be right
For sane people would never
Give in without a fight

Child-Like Mindset

I want to return to the little girl I once was
Carefree, energetic, and happy
I want to know how I lost this "child-like" mindset

As we age and grow, our hearts become less bright
Our minds become more dark
Our smiles begin to fade away

Why is this considered normal
Shouldn't we all strive to be like these children
Full of energy. Full of joy. Full of love.
Not caring how we are perceived, but simply
just... Being

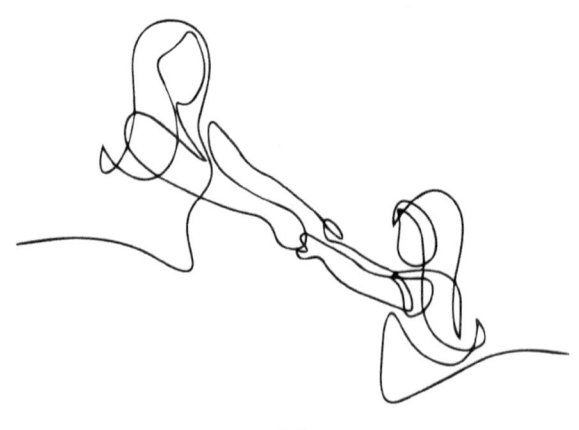

Your Love, My Mind

Your love is a paper cut
Causing searing pain
Hardly visible from outside
But a constant ache from within

Your love is a disease
Causing internal strife
I can't get rid of it
Even to save my life

Your love is a wildfire
Burning with rage
Setting alight my heart
With your steady outrage

I gloss over each problem as if it's not real
Because paper cuts seal
Diseases slowly heal
Wildfires destroy to reveal what's concealed

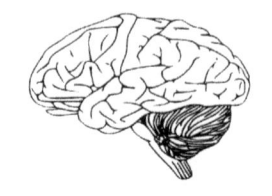

Her Eyes Are Green

Her eyes are green
Green like the underside of every leaf
Green like a lake when the sun reflects the trees just right
Not the deep green of emeralds, but the soft green of peridots
Green like the pale, lusciousness of pears
They captivate you and you become lost
Lost in memories of rolling fields and the breeze blowing in summer
Lost in every precious, beautiful, memorable thing in this world, because that is what she is
She is precious. She is beautiful. She is memorable.
Even if you were to never see her again, you would remember her every feature
Each freckle on her face. Each shape of her fingers. The way her mouth is always slightly curled into a smile

As if she found every aspect of life just as fascinating as she is

But most of all, you'll remember that her eyes are green

Haiku

My life is a lie

Constantly having to hide

The question is why

Perfectionist

No time to stop, no time to breathe

No time to eat, no time to sleep

The work is piled up in heaps

Yet you have to get it done

No simple days of relaxation

You don't have time for hesitation

"So what?" if there's no motivation

It's not supposed to be fun

Perfection is the way to go

Make sure everything you do it shows

And even if you're all alone

You'll at least be number one

Keep climbing if you're out of breath

Everyone must be impressed

Who cares if you have nothing left

It's only just begun

Water Pressure

Calm me, cover me, make me clean
Underneath the water is where I feel seen
This weight is something I've felt before
I'm already drowning, so what's a little more

It doesn't take much for me to give in
Lungs constricting again and again
Sinking further into the ocean's dark depths
Eternal sleep calls to me and I gladly accept

I'm Rotten Fruit

Love is so bitter

But that's why it's sweet

You can't help but savor

The fruit that you eat

It's rotten and molded

Covered in dirt

It's bruised and discarded

Because it's been hurt

If we take out its heart

That's been showered in tears

And replant it somewhere

It can grow for more years

Then this tangled-up mess

Of flayed skin and bone

Can grow into a tree

And finally find home

Stolen

In a grass-covered field laying under the stars

Your arms are my only shield

Tonight the world is no one's but ours

Let our love be revealed

Here we are free from oppression and stares

Our bodies out of reach

It's easy to see that this world is not fair

No matter what they preach

These moments are stolen, so we must be criminals

They try to lock us away

How can they think that this is forgivable

When they've caused us so much pain

Out here with you, I feel so alive

Shouting out to the night

In the enveloping dark is where we thrive

Though we wish to be in the light

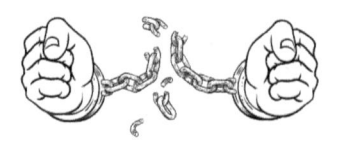

Polaroid

I have a million Polaroids

Hung across my room

Each on a unique reminder

Of times spent out with you

But these photographs don't capture

The shots behind the scenes

And it's so easy to forget

That life is never what it seems

I constantly romanticized

Something never real

The fantasies throughout my mind

Altered what I feel

The version of you in my head

Was perfect without fault

My expectations were set way too high

And caused our love to halt

I didn't mean to set my goals

Somewhere you'd never touch

Yet I knew that you would one day leave

Because I am too much

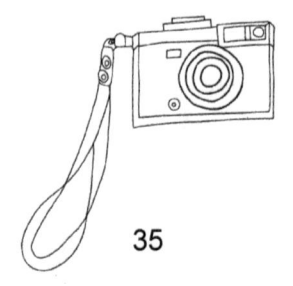

Printed in the USA
CPSIA information can be obtained
at www.ICGtesting.com
LVHW011244220224
772321LV00017BA/833